He went over a river.

He went up a hill.

He went into a wood.

9

He went behind a waterfall.

He went to the bin.

13

A Day Out

Bill
Bear
the bin
the footpath
the waterfall

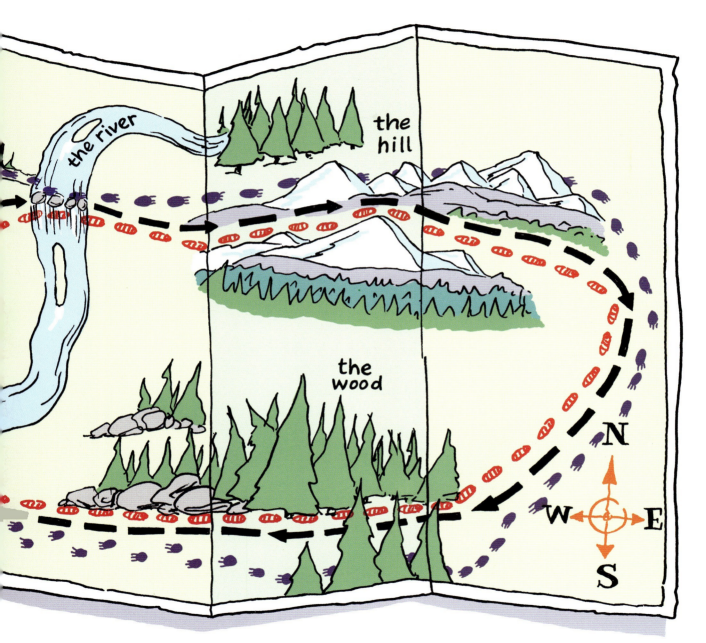

the river

the hill

the wood

N
W E
S

Ideas for reading

Written by Alison Tyldesley MA PGCE
Education, Childhood and Inclusion Lecturer

Reading objectives:

- read and understand simple sentences
- demonstrate understanding when talking with others about what they have read
- use phonic knowledge to decode regular words and read them aloud accurately

Communication and language objectives:

- listen to stories, accurately anticipating key events and respond to what they hear with relevant comments, questions or actions
- express themselves effectively, showing awareness of listeners' needs
- develop their own narratives and explanations by connecting ideas or events

Curriculum links: Knowledge and Understanding of the World

words: a, for, he, went, to, up

Interest words: over, into, behind

Word count: 30

Build a context for reading

- Look carefully at the front cover. Encourage the children to spot important details like the bear and the litter bin. Read the title together.
- Walk through the book, looking at the pictures. Leave pp14–15 until later. Ask the children what happens to the man and the bear.
- Discuss the fact that the pictures extend the story told by the words (you have to 'read' the pictures too).
- Ask the children to point to the words on p2 and read them carefully, making a one-to-one match.
- Look more carefully at the picture on p3 and ask the children to describe exactly what is happening.

Understand and apply reading strategies

- Ask the children to read the book aloud and independently up to p13. Prompt and praise correct pointing and matching of spoken and written words.
- Encourage the children to discuss the pictures as well as the text. What is happening? What is the bear thinking about?
- When you've read the story, look at pp14–15. Ask the children to point to each place and recall what happens in sequence.

Tapping in the Garden

Written by Samantha Eardley

Illustrated by Diobelle Cerna

Collins

tapping in the bedroom

a moonlit night

tapping in the bedroom

a moonlit night

tapping in the garden

a fantastic backpack

tapping in the garden

a fantastic backpack

tapping in a top hat

10

weeping dad

tapping in a top hat

weeping dad

 Review: After reading

Use your assessment from hearing the children read to choose any GPCs, words or tricky words that need additional practice.

Read 1: Decoding

- Use grapheme cards to make any words you need to practise. Model reading those words, using teacher-led blending.
- Ask the children to follow as you read the whole book, demonstrating fluency and prosody.

Read 2: Vocabulary

- Look back through the book and discuss the pictures. Encourage the children to talk about details that stand out for them. Use a dialogic talk model to expand on their ideas and recast them in full sentences as naturally as possible.
- Work together to expand vocabulary by naming objects in the pictures that children do not know.
- On page 7, discuss the meaning of **fantastic**. Ask: Why is the backpack fantastic? (e.g. *it is colourful and has a fun pattern on it*) What fantastic things have you got or seen? Why are they fantastic?

Read 3: Comprehension

- Discuss any tap dancing or other types of dancing the children have seen or done. Ask: What sort of dancing do you like best? Why? Do you think learning to dance takes lots of practice? Why?
- Talk about the end of the story. Ask: How do you think Dad felt? (e.g. *proud, happy*) How do you know? (e.g. *he wept*) Why do you think he was proud? (e.g. *he knew how hard the boy had practised*)
- Turn to pages 14 and 15 and talk about the different places where the story was set. Ask questions about each picture, for example: Where was he tapping at night? (*in the bedroom*) Where did he tap next? (*in the garden in the rain*) Where did he dance last of all? (*on a stage, in front of an audience*)

Bill went for a walk.

A Day Out

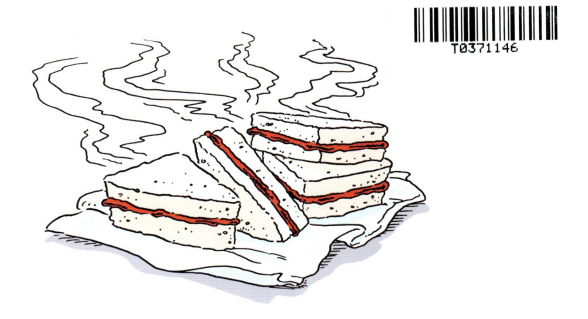

Written by Claire Llewellyn

Illustrated by Andy Hammond

Collins